Significant Aspects of Client-Centered Therapy

(A Psychology Classic)

Carl Rogers

CONTENTS

"We regard the medical model as an extremely inappropriate model for dealing with psychological disturbances. The model that makes more sense is a growth model or a developmental model. In other words we see people as having a potential for growth and development and that can be released under the right psychological climate. We don't see them as sick and needing a diagnosis, a prescription and a cure; and that is a very fundamental difference with a good many implications."

(Carl Rogers)

A Word From The Editor

Hello, a very warm welcome and many thanks for your interest in the psychology classic - "Significant Aspects of Client-Centered Therapy." My name is David Webb and I've had a passionate interest in psychology for over 20 years. I began studying psychology in 1990, and I've been teaching psychology in some capacity or another since 1998.

Widely regarded as one of the most influential psychologists of all time, Carl Rogers was a towering figure within the humanistic movement towards person centered theory and non-directive psychotherapy. Originally published in 1946 his classic article Significant Aspects of Client-Centered Therapy is essential reading for anybody interested in psychotherapy and counseling. In this landmark publication Carl Rogers outlines the origins of client-centered therapy, the process of client-centered therapy, the discovery and capacity of the client and the client-centered nature of the therapeutic relationship.

The Psychology Classics Initiative:

In recognition of the fact that there is absolutely no substitute for understanding and engaging with the issues under review than by reading the authors unabridged ideas, thoughts and findings in their entirety; Significant Aspects of Client-Centered Therapy has been produced as part of the psychology classics initiative to make important, insightful and engaging publications widely available.

How is This Possible?

Any book, magazine, journal or periodical published 1923 through 1963 whose copyright was not renewed in its 28th year is in the public domain. Every effort has been made to ensure that all the articles featuring in the psychology classics series are now in the public domain due to copyright expiration.

Bonus Material:

Significant Aspects of Client-Centered Therapy builds upon some of Carl Rogers' previously published work. Among the most notable of these earlier works were *The Processes of Therapy* and *The Development of Insight in A Counseling Relationship*; both of which are also presented in full.

Connect & Learn

Before you begin reading please take a moment to join me and thousands of psychology students online.

Psychology on Facebook

www.facebook.com/psychologyonline

Psychology on Twitter

https://twitter.com/psych101

Psychology on Google+

bit.ly/PsychologyGooglePlus

Psychology on Linkedin

http://bit.ly/PsychStudentsNetwork

Psychology on YouTube

www.youtube.com/user/LearnAboutPsychology

Psychology on Pinterest

pinterest.com/psychology/

And please feel free to explore the four websites built around my teaching and research interests.

www.all-about-psychology.com

www.all-about-forensic-psychology.com

www.all-about-forensic-science.com

www.all-about-body-language.com

Kind regards.

David Webb BSc (hons), MSc

The Processes of Therapy

Classic article from 1940 in which Rogers outlines the conditions for successful psychotherapy. Namely; rapport, free expression of feeling on the part of the client, recognition and acceptance by the client of his spontaneous self, responsible choices, the gaining of insight through assimilated interpretation and independence with support.

Recent years have brought significant progress in the field of psychotherapy. The help obtained by the individual in a series of treatment interviews is no longer a vague mystery impossible of serious investigation. Social workers, psychiatrists, and clinical psychologists working in this field have developed an increased understanding of the therapeutic process, and a greater degree of assurance in its use. The time is perhaps ripe for various workers to endeavor to formulate and describe the fundamental aspects of this process, in order that such descriptions may serve as hypotheses to be tested by research. This paper is an attempt to present such an analysis of the process of therapy. The ideas expressed are drawn from many sources, particularly from those with actual experience in treatment work.

Before a person can receive help from a therapist or counselor, it is essential that certain basic conditions be met. It is probably necessary that the client, whether child or adult, should feel some dissatisfaction with present adjustment, some fundamental need of help. Other treatment techniques, such as changes in the environment, may be effective without this feeling of need, but therapy, as the word has come to be used, can scarcely take place without it. Likewise, therapy has no chance of being successful if there

8

is too heavy a weight of adverse social factors making adjustment impossible except through radical alteration of circumstances. It is also necessary that the client have intelligence above the borderline level. These would seem to be the essential conditions for therapy. Research upon each of these points would be most helpful in determining the range of situations in which psychotherapy may be effective.

Granted these conditions, and a skilled therapist whose purpose is to release and strengthen the individual, rather than to intervene in his life, certain processes seem to take place, or if they do not take place, therapy is likely to be unsuccessful. These processes are described below. It should be noted that there is overlapping between these steps, and they do not always occur in the order in which they are set forth. The experiences described might be differently formulated or placed in different categories by some other therapist. Yet in most successful therapeutic experiences, where the individual leaves the contacts more able to handle his own problems, it is the writer's opinion that each of these steps will have been fulfilled.

I. Rapport is established:

There must be a warmth of relationship between counselor and counselee if any progress is to be made. Interviewing "tricks" will not do. There must be on the part of the counselor a genuine interest in the individual, a degree of identification which is none the less real because it is understood and to some extent controlled. Identification and objectivity are delicately balanced components in the counselor's approach.

In successful therapy these attitudes on the part of the therapist help to build up in the client the confidence and trust which make possible the subsequent elements in the process. The rapport which is established is a lasting thing throughout therapy, and constitutes a personal bond which needs to be gradually broken at the conclusion of the interviews. While its emotional value for the client is much greater than for the therapist, yet both are involved and do much better to admit this involvement frankly.

II. There is free expression of feeling on the part of the client:

Some of our most significant recent advances in therapy have been in this area. The values of catharsis, of release of feeling, have long been recognized, but only recently have we learned new ways of encouraging such release. The development of play therapy which uses all sorts of media for expression, and the development of psychodramatics are indications that we have only begun to discover the possible procedures in this field. In interview techniques progress has also been made so that we tend to avoid that blocking of free expression which is so characteristic of our older case records. It is worth noting that some schools of thought encourage expression of material related to past experience, others material related to present feelings. There seems to be no evidence that one is more therapeutic than the other, since, m an important sense, "all roads lead to Rome." Our most profound emotional patterns are as evident in our daily experience as in our past history, as plain in the immediate counseling relationship as in our childhood reactions.

III. Recognition and acceptance, by the client, of his spontaneous self:

This process is so closely interrelated with the previous one that they might almost be classed together. As material is given by the client, it is the therapist's function to help him recognize and clarify the emotions which he feels. In the rapport situation, where he is accepted rather than criticized, the individual is free to see himself without defensiveness, and gradually to recognize and admit his real self with its childish patterns, its aggressive feelings, and its ambivalences, as well as its mature impulses, and rationalized exterior. Often this recognition of self is achieved almost spontaneously, the therapist's only contribution having been to verbalize the feelings which are expressed in words or behavior or play activities. This process is very much akin to insight, except that it is on a basis of feeling, whereas the term insight is apt to have more of an intellectual connotation.

IV. The making of responsible choices:

Perhaps the sharpest difference between present day psychotherapy and earlier practice, is the degree to which the responsibility for the client's life is left in his own hands. The therapist at his best does not suggest, advise, or persuade. He does not assume responsibility for the client's decisions. Instead he encourages the individual, now more clearly aware of his true feelings, and with more acceptance of his total self, to take the responsibility for making new choices. Often hesitantly, often fearfully, the client does so, and is cheered and encouraged by the fact that he finds he can successfully take responsibility for himself, and can direct his energies toward new, self-chosen goals.

In actual therapeutic work there is something exciting and dramatic in these initial decisions, this growth toward independence, which visibly takes Place in the therapeutic relationship. From the point of view of psychological theory, however, it is not so difficult to explain. It is a good example of "learning through doing." Whereas older therapies, relying on intellectual insight and personal influence, hoped that the patient might alter his ways outside of the treatment relationship, the newer therapy gives opportunity for the practice of independent choices, greater responsibility, while still supported by the rapport situation. Thus there is much greater "transfer of training" to other life situations.

V. The gaining of insight through assimilated interpretation:

The foundation of insight seems to be the emotional acceptance of self mentioned under III. In addition, however, insight is often enriched by the therapist's interpretation of emotional patterns in the life of the individual which have not been recognized. Such interpretations, largely explanations of motives for behavior, serve no useful purpose, and may retard progress, if they are not accepted by the client. Hence, the use of the term "assimilated interpretation." Although this process has deep roots in Freudian psychoanalytic procedures, it is probably much less used than formerly. It is the one process described which may play very little, if any, part.

We undoubtedly owe much to Rank and Jung for the declining emphasis on insight alone. Insight plus responsible, self-directed choices toward new goals produces new and effective integration. Insight alone, as we see from some of the personal accounts of analysis in the Journal of Abnormal and Social Psychology, may leave the individual wiser, but little better able to cope with his situation.

VI. Growing into independence with support:

The final period of any therapeutic experience is the process of education or re-education which makes possible the effective continuance of the fundamental gains which have been made. In choosing new goals, the client may need new information which the therapist may supply or help him to obtain. In taking independent steps to cope with his adjustment problems, there will be discouragements and defeats, which the rapport situation helps to neutralize. In these new experiences there are fresh opportunities for the client to see himself even more clearly and to make use of the insight he has previously gained. If the initial aspects of therapy have been successful, this final period comes to a close quite naturally, with some feeling of loss on both sides to be sure, but with the client's feeling of assurance that he can now handle his situation alone.

These are suggested as the basic elements of psychotherapy as we now know it whether applied to nursery age children or gray-haired adults. While there is something very unsatisfactory in stripping therapy of the subtle nuances and dramatic elements which assuredly belong to it and presenting only the bare bones of therapeutic process, it is a necessary task if we are to make progress. The finest touches of artistry will not make counseling contacts helpful if they are basically unsound in principle. It is to attempt to give one formulation to these basic principles that this article has been written.

In closing, attention might be called to the research opportunities with which the therapeutic process bristles. There is the need of adequate records - stenographic, even phonographic - upon which comprehensive study may be based. There is the question of accessibility for therapy. Can we draw a line between those who would profit, and those who might be better helped by other treatment procedures?

There is the need for both imagination and research in the field of expression. Are the same basic feelings expressed in dreams, in play materials, in dramatic constructions, in verbalizations? There is need for much more study of the give and take of the interviewing process. How is expression encouraged, how may interpretations be made, how may the therapeutic progress be accelerated through the interview? There is the need for translating individual therapy into group procedures, to make it more widely helpful. There is the need for much more refined analysis of processes in therapy based on a study of complete records and formulated in terms of known psychological facts.

If clinical and applied psychology is to win the status it desires, if it is to find sound answers to the problems of human relationships which are so urgently needed in a distraught world, then it will need to promote much more study and effort than heretofore, in this dynamic field of therapy.

The Development of Insight In A Counseling Relationship

Classic counseling paper in which Carl Rogers addresses the question of how an individual client may come to an effective understanding of himself/herself.

In dealing with adolescent and adult clients, one question which faces the worker - whether psychologist, case worker, psychiatrist, or educational counselor - is, "How may this individual come to an effective understanding of himself?" It is recognized that once the individual genuinely understands his behavior, and accepts that understanding, he is able to adopt a more realistic and satisfactory control of his actions, is less likely to hurt others to gain satisfactions, and in general can become more mature. But how to reach this goal?

This understanding of self we customarily call insight. We find rather general agreement that the achievement of insight is the keystone of the process of therapy. Whether we are dealing with a student who is maladjusted, or a marriage which is skidding toward failure, or a war neurosis, the essentials of a therapeutic experience seem to be the same. First comes the experience of release - the pouring out of feelings, the loosening of repressions, the unburdening of guilt, the lessening of tension. There follows, if progress is to be made, the understanding of self, the acceptance of one's impulses, the perception of relationships, which we classify under the term insight. Then, out of this more accurate view of the inner life, out of this new understanding of the web of personal adjustments, come new plans, new choices, new and more satisfying ways of meeting the realities with which the individual is faced. While each of these three steps is essential, and no one can take place without the other, the middle step, the achievement of insight, is a crucial one and deserves much more attention than it has had in the past.

In the counseling and the research on counseling which is being carried forward at Ohio State, we are gradually accumulating more information about this important aspect of psychotherapy. We are finding that in counseling relationships governed by a non-directive viewpoint, highly significant insights develop with a spontaneity and vigor which is astonishing [3]. We are also becoming more and more convinced, though, as yet research evidence is meagre, that such spontaneous insight is not characteristic of other counseling approaches. We find that the directive procedures which are characteristic of so much educational guidance do not produce insight of this sort. Our evidence would also point to the conclusion that spontaneous insight is a rare occurrence in the more interpretative approaches such as psychoanalysis. Consequently, it appears to be worthwhile to present both examples and research evidence regarding the achievement of self-understanding as we are seeing it.

Insight, as it is coming to be defined through our practical experience and research findings, involves such elements as (1) an acceptance of one's impulses and attitudes, good or bad, including attitudes previously repressed; (2) an understanding of the patterning of one's behavior, the perception of new relationships; (3) a fresh perception of reality made possible by this acceptance and understanding of the self; (4) the planning of new and more satisfying ways in which the self can adjust to reality. Since this definition grows out of examination of the data, not from armchair speculation, an attempt will be made to let the data speak for themselves.

16

Where problems are not too deep seated, simple and partial insights may come very quickly. A father, concerned about his ten-year-old daughter, is encouraged to talk out his attitudes, and arrives at these insightful reactions in a single interview [4].

Father: She's awful pokey - awful pokey. You just can't get her going. Of course, maybe it's been our fault. It's been easier to do things for her than to teach her to do them. She hasn't enough to do. She ought to have more responsibility.

Counselor: That's a splendid idea...You feel you haven't given her a chance to learn?

Father: Yes. She gets an allowance, but the trouble is she spends it. And then It comes time to go to the show and she hasn't any. And I haven't the heart - I give it to her. (Pause) Of course when I was a boy I didn't have any money at all - I had to earn everything.

Counselor: You think it would have been better if someone had given it to you?

Father: Well, it wouldn't have hurt. My parents could have...(Pause) I know I give in to her and she knows it, see?

This may seem like a minimum degree of insight. It could be briefly stated in these terms "She should have more responsibility, but I don't give it to her because I feel sorry for myself as a boy." It is a simple insight, yet it is effective. Before the father leaves he says, in a hesitating manner, "I kinda think tomorrow morning when she wakes up she's going to find she has some things to do!" One year later the school principal, talking to the psychologist about this child, knowing nothing of the above, says, "Well, she seems bet-

17

ter...And the attitude of the parents seems different. They seem to be giving her more responsibility in various ways." This illustrates one of the points which I would like to make-that partial insights, spontaneously arrived at, are surprisingly effective in bringing about alteration of behavior.

Another illustration of such simple and partial insight might be given. A young bride has been troubled by guilt feelings about an experience previous to her marriage in which she had been intensely in love with a young man who regarded her as "just a passing fancy." She is troubled about keeping this experience from her husband. She talks out her attitudes in one contact, getting considerable release. In a second brief contact she shows how much insight she has gained.

I guess I needed to talk to someone about it. I think I can see where I stand now. If I were to tell Nick it would merely mean that I was selfish. I would be telling him to help myself, not because of anything I feel I owe to him. It would be 'passing the buck' to him. I see now that it was merely an experience that hurt me - hurt my ego. It's only natural that I should feel queer about it. But that feeling queer is my own burden. Certainly it's unfair to pass it on to Nick. It would certainly be foolish of me to endanger our relationship, too. Time will cure my 'conditioning' to this very small unpleasant segment of my life - and my marital happiness will hasten this time. I already feel my perspective changing - the present looms larger and larger and the rest dwindles.

Here we find that the insight achieved involves a better acceptance of attitudes previously denied-the hurt to her ego - a clearer perception of the patterning and significance of her own desire to tell her husband, and finally a choice of a new method of handling the problem.

18

As might be expected, a working insight is not always so easily achieved. Much depends on the complexity of the problem, and the extent to which attitudes are repressed. In the case of an aviation cadet who was failing in his solo flights, counseling brought to light an intense and hitherto denied hatred for his unreasonably strict father. The gradual perception of a relationship between his attitude toward his father and his reactions during his flights covers several interviews. Brief excerpts from the fifth, sixth, and tenth interviews will illustrate the development of this insight.

From fifth interview:

S. You know after the last interview I wondered what made me tell you the things that I did. Could it be possible that the instructor is a symbol of my father? Is that hatred coming back to blot my memory? Could that possibly be significant?

C. You wonder if perhaps the instructor might be a symbol of your father.

S. Yes, he was telling me what to do just like Dad always did. I fully intended to carry out the instructor's directions; I couldn't not want to do them. Maybe I forgot because I thought of Dad and wanted to forget.

From the sixth interview:

S. On the basis of what we've done thus far the instructor may have been considered in the role of my father and as he was telling me what to do I probably didn't want to because I thought of him as my father - but I don't know - I'm not sure.

C. You're not absolutely sure that that's the answer to your problem.

S. I'm not positive but that's what it seems to be at the present time. If you said it was I would know it. Then recognizing that fact, I wouldn't be bothered in the plane any more.

C. If I should say that was the solution to your problem and you didn't thoroughly believe it yourself, that wouldn't do much good, would it? Of if I told you that wasn't the solution to your problem, and you thought that perhaps it was, then my telling you wouldn't do a bit of good either.

S. (Smiling) I see your point. I guess you're right. From the tenth interview: The cadet tells of a recent failure to do well. The counselor recognizes his feeling.

C. You didn't follow his instructions up in the air even when he was telling you.

S. It seems that way. If you could apply that to other maneuvers it might be. I really want to fly though. Maybe that's why I haven't done so well - a dislike to follow directions. Gee, that's pretty well tangled up. Let me try and draw a parallel there. My instructor is to my father as my instructor's directions are to my father's directions. Even though I thought I wanted to, I really didn't want to.

C. You feel there's a parallel to your father's and instructor's directions.

S. I wanted to fly badly. That may be the block. That's probably the answer to the question. I guess I didn't have it formulated before I came here today, but I sure do now.

C. You feel that may be at the center of your problem. S. That's right. Flying is grand. By George, why did I have to get an instructor that reminded me of father? If I got an easy instructor all the way through would it have been easier? There's a good possibility I would have been the best in the group.

In this material the insight which is gained is primarily a new perception of relationships between past repressed attitudes and present experiences. It should be pointed out that neither in this case, nor in any of the cases cited in this paper, has the counselor ever suggested these insights in any way. The counseling has been non-directive, with the counselor reflecting, in an understanding fashion, the attitudes and feelings expressed. The understanding of self springs from the client, not from the counselor.

In other instances the insight consists largely of an acceptance of the denied portions of the self. Illustrations of this type of insight may be taken from the case of Mrs. S., a young, highly educated mother, who comes for assistance because she is having trouble with her child and is losing the affection of her husband. Some of the points at which she comes face to face with her own feelings may be given. First she faces her basic rejection of her child.

Mrs. S. I'm afraid I'd have to say this of myself, I really didn't want Buddy. We were married two years, and I had a job. My husband didn't want me to work. We thought children would be the best solution. We felt social pressure too. With the birth rate up in the lower groups, college graduates should have children. In a limited way we were emotionally interested in him, but not deeply. And I've never adjusted to having him! It's terrible to say this!

21

Later she sees the relationship of this rejection, and of her difficulty with her husband, to Buddy's behavior.

Mrs. S. He senses the tension in us, lacks security. That probably explains it all. I used to put myself into working for social causes. Now I've given myself all to my husband, none to Buddy. I pat him and tell him I love him, but I wonder if he doesn't know.

C. You feel perhaps he realizes you don't love him much.

Mrs. S. Say not til now. But with the situation as it is - how will it come?

C. You want to love him.

Mrs. S. Yes, very much. I'm not just coldblooded.

At another point she begins to accept the role of being a woman, rather than merely an intellectual. Talking about her husband, she says:

Mrs. S. I spend my time worrying about him, discussing with him his feelings and emotions. Instead I should take an interest in myself, my clothes, my hair. I've never been that sort of person - I hate to fuss with my hair. I shouldn't say that - after I'm through, and look in the mirror, I like myself better. That's the first time I've thought of it that way.

C. Instead of being tense about him, you feel you should take an interest in yourself, and you find that doing that, like fussing with your hair, is not as foreign to your nature as you thought.

Mrs. S. Yes. I have more hope now than I have felt to this moment.

In regard to her relationship to her husband, this woman also gains much, insight in which she sees the problem in a new frame of reference, and also decides what she can do about it.

Mrs. S. I'm more firmly convinced than ever that what I have to look at is myself,, rather than Bill, do something about my own faults and shortcomings. I thought a lot about it last night; I realized a person can only be responsible for oneself, not for the other person's feelings and emotions. I wasn't treating him as an individual - my emotional involvement makes that hard. I tried to think and feel for him, take over his problem and work it through for him.

C. Now you feel you can be responsible for yourself, and can let him be responsible for himself.

Mrs. S. Yes. Things may break down, but we can build them up again.

C. While things may not go smoothly, you feel more basic security.

Mrs. S. Yes. I've got to look to myself, to see how I'm dressing and behaving with him.

C. You feel those are your responsibility.

Mrs. S. Yes. And the children - I'm not excusing myself about them. I thought it was impossible for anyone to take care of a house, and herself, and find time to play with the children, but I think now I can. I'd assumed some things were impossible, but they were not.

In these excerpts, being able to accept as a part of herself her rejecting attitudes, and her desire to be a woman, enables her to achieve a more detached and realistic attitude toward the reality of her husband and his behavior. It also frees her to choose new patterns of reaction.

In the instances which have been given the insights which were achieved were relatively simple, though definitely significant. In some cases insights are much more involved, and the achievement of them is a more gradual process. A series of excerpts from the case of Alfred will indicate something of the richness which this insight process may have. Alfred was a very withdrawn student, the reclusive sort who was living largely in fantasy when he first came in. The possibility of a schizophrenic break seemed very real. There were twenty interviews, and during that period he altered in a most striking fashion in his behavior and attitudes. He became independent and socially adjusted, indeed something of a social leader. His adjustment has been further tested by two years in the army, to which he has reacted very well. There are in his case many threads of insight which would be intriguing to follow. One which has been selected is his gradual achievement of understanding of his daydreaming. His gropings toward this insight are a fascinating process to watch. It is unfortunate that only brief excerpts can be given from the phonographic recordings of the contacts.

In the seventh interview: Alfred first shows a real understanding of the fact that his daydreaming was compensatory.

Alfred. I always had the idea that I would make up for a lot of the things I didn't do - like being an Edison or a Lincoln

24

some day. Yet I never did enjoy the real happiness that kids were having at the present time. I always kidded myself along by thinking that 'I'm going to be a great man someday'. And when you get to college, and really find out how many brilliant people there are you realize you've been kidding yourself. You certainly never could become important if you were to go on in the past, instead of concentrating and studying and everything. I think maybe if I could be as happy as this I could amount to something - probably not an Edison or Lincoln, but I could hold a position. It would certainly be through an entirely different set of plans than I planned on the other way of doing it.

In the tenth interview he brings out more forcibly how much the fantasy meant to him, and how difficult has been the process of bringing it into the full light of consciousness.

Alfred. So anyway I do believe coming over here is helping me, because these things don't bother me as much as they used to. And I used to carry them around with me. For instance, that daydreaming. Boy, it just about killed me the first time I tried to tell that to anybody, but I suppose that if I tell it about twenty-five times I'll really begin to laugh at it.

In the eleventh interview he expands the insight gained. He is able to face the fact that the satisfactions of fantasy existed not only in the past, but even during the initial stages of counseling. He also faces frankly the fact that his fantasy goals are impossible.

Alfred. I just used to comfort myself at school by telling myself that I would be a very famous person some day, and I didn't just say that as a sort of compromise, I actually believed that that was right, and even when I was coming here I still did think that. I remember one time I said to myself,

'If I were happy I would be another Abe Lincoln', but if your mind is really normal and out in the world, you realize how really big the world is and you realize that maybe you aren't going to accomplish as much as you want.

In the fourteenth interview Alfred makes the final link in this chain of insight when he becomes genuinely willing to face and accept the prospect of being only an average person, in the real world, rather than a great person in a fantasy world of his own making.

Alfred. I might desire to be an awfully great person, but really just to be average and to be normal is something to be very appreciative of, because I was thinking it could very easily be that I could grow up to be a bum. I was watching some of the newsies, men about 35 or 40, selling their papers, and I thought, 'Gee, just to be average really isn't such a little thing.' For a man to have a respected position, he really doesn't need to be known even in his own community as a great figure, but to be average is really a very high position compared with how low a person could fall in the opposite direction where he would be a bum.

In these excerpts we see Alfred openly accepting his fantasies, and able to bring them fully into consciousness, recognizing that they are compensatory, recognizing that he has used them as a means of satisfaction right up to the present, perceiving the difference between fantasy satisfactions and the less glamorous but more substantial satisfactions of real goals, and finally accepting a realistic goal as his own. This is a rich, deep, and thoroughly effective instance of spontaneous insight.

In this same case there is still another thread of insight which is worthy of our attention. He was, as has been mentioned, a very withdrawn young man, with no satisfying contacts of a social nature, standing on the brink of creating his own private world in the form of a psychosis. A few of his statements, as he comes to see himself more clearly in this respect, will both illustrate the achievement of insight, and reveal the way the world looks to a highly reclusive individual. During the seventh interview he indicates something of his isolation, and the dawning realization that he might be able to deal with it.

Alfred. It's like a curtain in a theatre, something that shuts me off from the players in the rest of the play. Just completely isolates me. Until I pull that curtain away and look at myself as being one of the players the same as anyone else, I won't be able to get very far. At times when I really get to looking at these things the way I should, I wonder why I don't jump in and get in the stream of life.

In the eleventh interview he begins to see this isolation as being partially in the past, giving a vivid picture of the way he felt. He also recognizes that he is changing, living more in a world of social reality.

Alfred. I just withdrew a little more each year until things had gotten to a point that around Christmas time I started to wonder for fear I was the only person that was alive. I must have gotten away from the present world that much, that everything just kind of disappeared, kinda, and I felt as if I were standing on a hill all alone or something, and everything was gone, and here I was all alone. But the more I start going back in the group, why - I know the other day I was thinking about something, I don't know, I had my mind on something else, and I suddenly got the idea, 'Well, how in the world could I have gotten the idea that I was the only

27

person existing. Here this person is every bit the same as I am.'

As might be supposed, it is not an easy matter to face all these deep problems within the self, and reorient to new goals, yet growth was steadily made during the interviews. In the sixteenth interview Alfred gives a picture of the two opposing forces within himself, the desire for growth and the desire to withdraw from life. His description of the constructive turmoil into which his life has been thrown has the genuine literary quality which only accompanies a struggle to say deeply significant things.

Alfred. I certainly think in a way the problem is a lot clearer than a while ago, yet - maybe - It's like the ice breaking up on a pond in the spring, it's - while things are a lot nearer to - While the pond is a lot nearer to being nothing but clear water, yet things are much more unstable now, possibly, than when the pond was, covered over with ice. What I'm trying to bring out is that I seem to be so much in a terrible fog all of the time lately, but I do feel a lot better off than I was before, because then I didn't even realize what was the matter. But maybe all this fog and so-called trouble is due to the fact of two opposing forces in me now. You know it's not really a case of just letting one be superior, but it's kinda breaking up and reorganizing that's going on now that makes things seem so doubly bad. So maybe I'm better off than I think.

The person who is skilled in therapy will realize that this is a deep and genuine insight, and will not be surprised that in the next interview Alfred made a definite decision to obtain a job as junior counselor in a summer camp, a step he had contemplated before, but about which he had been unable to come to a clear decision.

In this second train of insightful thinking, which could be illustrated with many other examples from the recordings, Alfred sees clearly his icebound, frozen, isolated personality, and comes to see also the attractiveness of life in a social, real, world. Though he also perceives the pain and difficulty of such a radical reorganization of life, he is able to face this and to take steps in the direction of social life and social responsibility.

As may have been noted, these spontaneous insights, wrought out of the individual's struggle to see himself more clearly, have a depth and a sincerity and an individual quality which are quite lacking in attempts on the part of the counselor to "give" the client insight. This is the person seen from within, rather than without, and the difference is very striking. As an illustration of the attempt to give insight, a portion may be taken from an electrically recorded psychoanalysis, conducted by a reputable psychoanalyst. This example could be duplicated hundreds of times in the course of the 424 interviews of the analysis.

The patient, a schizophrenic young man, has been telling, in the fourth interview, about vaguely guilty feelings which he had while in the cafeteria, and the thought that if he did not eat much for lunch, he could later go to the candy counter, but then remarks that these ideas are foolish. The interview continues:

Analyst. What does eating candy make you think of?

Patient. Home, right away now. That's what it means.

Analyst. And what does home make you think of?

Patient. My mother.

Analyst. And what does your mother make you think of?
Patient. Oh, children, babies. Those ideas are put in my head. I don't know. I've got those thoughts again in my head.

Analyst. Yes. And as you think of babies, what comes into your mind.

Patient. Girls, I guess. Barbara Royce.

Analyst. Barbara Royce?

Patient. Yes. (very long pause).

Analyst. You see, you have guilt about Barbara Royce. You undoubtedly have sex feelings about her and something within yourself has been trying to convince you that this is wrong. That same part of your personality is making you feel guilty about eating, about going down to the cafeteria, about asking for a second course, about eating candy. You see, it connects right up with the thoughts that come, that somehow you - one part of you is trying to make you believe that all of that is wrong. Well, we know it isn't. (Pause) Why shouldn't you feel that way toward girls?

Patient. Well, I don't see any reason why I shouldn't. That's just a - Well, it's all right. (Long pause.)

Here it seems all too clear that any seeing of relationships, any perception of pattern, is in the mind of the analyst, not in the mind of the patient. The nearest he comes to accepting his own feelings is a passive acceptance of the analyst's attitude, by saying, "Well, it's all right." This is pale indeed alongside of the spontaneous insights which we have been examining. It lacks any of the internal conviction which they

30

carry. It shows how weak are attempts to give insight, when compared with the client's achievement of insight.

Our knowledge regarding insight comes not only from such examples as have been given, but from research studies which have been made. Three of these investigations have findings pertinent to the topic of insight. Snyder [5] has made an objective study of the characteristics of non-directive counseling in six complete counseling cases. He devised an objective list of 38 carefully defined categories and classified each of the nearly 10,000 client and counselor responses into one of these categories, thus making possible a statistical study of the counseling process. Raimy [2] has studied the changing concepts of the self which the individual exhibits in counseling. His study is based on 14 recorded cases. Curran [1] has made an exhaustive analysis of the case of Alfred, with particular reference to the problem of insight. From these three studies certain findings in regard to self - understanding in non - directive counseling may be briefly stated, with the source in parenthesis.

1. Insight primarily follows outpourings of material with a negative emotional content, colored by such attitudes as hostility, self criticism, and hopelessness. (Curran, 1.)

2. Insightful responses are most likely to follow immediately upon counselor responses of simple acceptance. They tend not to follow interpretation, persuasion, or other directive counselor responses. (Snyder, 5.)

3. An important aspect of insight is the seeing of relationships between issues heretofore regarded as unrelated. (Curran, 1.)

4. Another important aspect of insight is the alteration of concepts of the self. Individuals who come for counseling tend to see themselves in a strongly negative light as worthless, bad, inferior, etc. As insight is gained and the self is accepted, the self-concept is reorganized and a strong positive valuation is placed on it. The individual sees himself in much more positive terms. (Raimy, 2.)

5. As insight is gained into given problems or issues, those problems tend to drop out of the client's conversation. (Curran, 1.)

6. Insight and the making of independent plans and decisions both constitute a very small fraction of the client's conversation at the outset of counseling, but rise to become a significant part of the concluding interviews. These two categories taken together constitute 12.5 per cent of the client responses in initial interviews, 30.5 per cent of the middle interviews, and 42.5 per cent of the final counseling interviews. (Snyder, 5.)

With the evidence thus far given, indicating that spontaneous insights do occur in non-directive counseling, that they exhibit themselves in a variety of ways, and that they are significant in altering the client's concept of himself and his way of behaving, it becomes important to ask ourselves, Under what conditions is this spontaneous insight most likely to be achieved?

A careful examination of a growing body of data brings one to the conclusion that there is one primary principle operative. When the client is freed from all need of being in any way defensive, spontaneous insight comes bubbling through into consciousness. When the client is talking through his problems in an atmosphere in which all his attitudes are

32

genuinely understood and accepted, and in which there is nothing to arouse his desire to protect himself, insight develops.

Some workers will feel disappointed in the simplicity of this conclusion. They will feel that they have always dealt with clients in an accepting fashion. The fact is however that most of the procedures actually used in counseling contacts are such as to make clients defensive. This is clearly shown by our study of recorded interviews. It is not enough for the worker to have an accepting attitude, though this is important. The techniques used must also be such that defensiveness will not be aroused. Let us look at some of the methods actually employed by most workers.

Questions, for example, constitute one of the methods most frequently used in counseling. They may be simple questions such as, "When was that?" "Did he like it?" Or they may constitute an attempt to get deeper into attitudes expressed by asking, "Why did you feel that way about it?" "Why did you think that was bad?" "Why do you think these things happen?" Or questions may be of a highly probing nature, "What did you think about your mother?" "Will you behave next time the way you did this time?" In varying degrees all these questions arouse the psychological defenses of the client. There is always the fear that the questions may go too far, may uncover the attitudes which the client is afraid to reveal even to himself. Snyder's study showed that counselor questions tend to be followed frequently by rejection of the question by the client.

Evaluative responses are another familiar aspect of counseling. We have learned long ago that negative evaluations - comments which imply criticism, which question motives, which pass judgment on the client-tend to freeze the situation, and to make spontaneous expression difficult. We have not sufficiently learned that reassurance, agreement, and commendation have the same effect to a lesser degree. "I agree with, you," "You're certainly right,' "You've done very well," "You don't need to feel guilty about that," are the sort of well-intentioned comments which actually make it more difficult for the client to bring contradictory attitudes into the relationship. They show that the counselor is passing judgment on the client. These particular attitudes are judged favorably but the client fears that there may be attitudes which will be judged unfavorably, and hence is unable to bring his thinking fully into the interview.

Advice and suggestions are, we know, freely given even by those who protest strongly that they do not wish to guide the client's life. "Of course you will want to make your own decision, but I think you might try . . . " is one of the many subtle ways by which we introduce our own solutions to the client's problems. Such procedures cut off free expression. In two ways they make the client defensive. If he brings out deeper attitudes it would seem to imply that the counselor had not solved the problem. It would also bring the possibility that the counselor would try to solve these deeper problems in ways which the client did not want.

Interpretation of the client to himself is a technique used somewhat by psychologists and social workers, and very heavily by psychiatrists and analysts. The more shrewd the interpretation, the more it hits the mark, the greater the defensiveness it arouses, unless the client has already reached that point of insight himself. Snyder found that interpretation, even when made by skilled counselors, is most likely to be followed by client responses which deny the interpretation. The client is thrown on the defensive.

34

To sum it up, most of the procedures which we customarily use in counseling tend to put the client subtly on his guard. As we analyze our psychotherapeutic contacts there are only two techniques which are actually in accord with the accepting viewpoint which most workers profess. These are simple acceptance - " Yes," "M-hm," "I understand" - and recognition and clarification of feeling. The first needs no explanation, but there is no doubt that it serves an important part in developing a permissive atmosphere where the client can discover insight.

The procedure of recognizing and clarifying attitudes is one which also has a deceptive simplicity. It consists in mirroring, reflecting for the client the feelings he has been expressing, often more clearly than he has been able to do for himself. Two examples might be given. The first one is a very simple reflection of a straightforward attitude, taken from the case of the aviation cadet mentioned earlier.

Cadet. I should have soloed long ago. And here is something. Before I joined the Navy I was an overhead electrical crane operator, and that takes depth perception, coordination, and alertness; and I'm positive that I can apply that to my flying.

Counselor. You feel that your training as a crane operator should help you in your flying.

Cadet. That's right And here's something else...

This simple recognition of feeling serves the purpose of making expression of attitude easy, and of interposing nothing which will make the client in any way defensive. It makes him feel that he is understood, and enables him to go on to another area of emotionalized attitude, until gradually he has worked into the deeper and really significant realms.

Responses which might be termed clarification serve a further purpose of assisting the client to understand himself, but without any trace of an approach which would, arouse defensiveness. A brief example from a case in which the man was disturbed over his tendency to gamble excessively will illustrate this point.

Mr. R. One thing I have thought of vaguely, that might be the cause of everything; I have had the props knocked out from under me so many times since I went into business. After I got out of the University I went into business in L - , and had a good practice there, but my family didn't want me to stay there. They kept after me until I gave it up and came home. I worked for my father then, and had just gotten up to a decent job when I was let out for no particular reason. Next time I set up a lease that was profitable, and just at the time when I was about ready to profit from it, they cancelled the lease.

Counselor. You feel that the breaks have been against you.

Here the counselor's response puts briefly, and in clearer form, the underlying attitude which the client has been expressing. It is as such recognition and clarification of feeling frees the client from all need for defense, since it never in any way attacks the ego, that expression becomes freer, deeper attitudes are brought forth, and insights are developed. The justification for the development of these non-directive attitudes, and the skills which implement them, lie in the results which they bring.

This material has certain clear implications for the worker who deals with maladjusted clients in need of help. If deeper degrees of insight are deemed desirable, if it is important that the client reorganize his concept of himself, if he needs to find fresh and more satisfying ways of dealing with his problem, then the worker will increase the likelihood of this by adopting certain view points and procedures. The worker will need to cultivate a tolerant, accepting attitude which quite genuinely accepts the individual as he is. Furthermore the worker will need to utilize in the counseling situation only those techniques, which prevent defensiveness from arising. Aside from simple acceptance, the major technique is that of mirroring for the client the emotionalized attitude which he is expressing. Snyder found that these two types of responses constituted nearly 75 per cent of the counselor's statements in non-directive counseling. Their use and the counselor's accepting attitude are undoubtedly the primary reason for the development of the spontaneous insights which have been discussed, insights which deeply alter the client's way of living.

SUMMARY

1. It has been found that in counseling situations of a non-directive character, new perceptions and understandings of self develop in spontaneous fashion.

2. These insights are of various types, some relatively simple, some highly complex and going to the root of the behavior patterns of the individual.

3. Research shows that these insights develop gradually in a non-directive counseling situation and mount to a peak toward the conclusion of the counseling experience. They follow free expression of negative emotion. They are closely connected with a, positive change in the self concept. They are accompanied or followed by plans and decisions which involve the alteration of behavior.

4. Insights are not likely to follow counselor procedures "which evaluate, question, probe, advise or interpret. They are likely to develop if the counselor uses responses which are accepting and clarifying. Procedures which make defensiveness on the part of the client completely unnecessary, but which make the client feel that lie is deeply understood, are most successful.

REFERENCES

1. Curran, Chas. A. An Analysis of a Process of Therapy Through Counseling and its Implications for a Philosophy of Personality. Unpublished Ph.D. thesis, the Ohio State University, Columbus, Ohio, 1944.

2. Raimy, Victor C. The Self-Concept as a Factor in Counseling and Personality Organization. Unpublished Ph.D. thesis, the Ohio State University, Columbus, Ohio, 1943.

3. Rogers, Carl R. Counseling and Psychotherapy Boston: Houghton Mifflin, 1942.

4. Sargent, Helen. "Non-directive Counseling Applied to a Single Interview," JOURNAL OF CONSULTING PSYCHOLOGY, 1943, 7: 186.

5. Snyder, Wm. U. An Investigation of the Nature of Non-Directive Psychotherapy. Unpublished Ph.D. thesis, The Ohio State University, Columbus, Ohio, 1943. A condensation of this thesis is shortly to be published in the Journal of General Psychology.

Significant Aspects of Client-Centered Therapy

As mentioned earlier, this Carl Rogers classic is a must read for anybody interested in psychotherapy and counseling. In this landmark publication Carl Rogers outlines the origins of client-centered therapy, the process of client-centered therapy, the discovery and capacity of the client and the client-centered nature of the therapeutic relationship.

In planning to address this group, I have considered and discarded several possible topics. I was tempted to describe the process of non-directive therapy and the counselor techniques and procedures which seem most useful in bringing about this process. But much of this material is now in writing. My own book on counseling and psychotherapy contains much of the basic material, and my recent more popular book on counseling with returning servicemen tends to supplement it. The philosophy of the client-centered approach and its application to work with children is persuasively presented by Allen. The application to counseling of industrial employees is discussed in the volume by Cantor. Curran has now published in book form one of the several research studies which are throwing new light on both process and procedure. Axline is publishing a book on play and group therapy. Snyder is bringing out a book of cases. So it seems unnecessary to come a long distance to summarize material which is, or soon will be obtainable in written form.

Another tempting possibility, particularly in this setting, was to discuss some of the roots from which the client-centered approach has sprung. It would have been interesting to show how in its concepts of repression and release, in its

39

stress upon catharsis and insight, it has many roots in Freudian thinking, and to acknowledge that indebtedness. Such an analysis could also have shown that in its concept of the individual's ability to organize his own experience there is an even deeper indebtedness to the work of Rank, Taft, and Allen. In its stress upon objective research, the subjecting of fluid attitudes to scientific investigation, the willingness to submit all hypotheses to a verification or disproof by research methods, the debt is obviously to the whole field of American psychology, with its genius for scientific methodology. It could also have been pointed out that although everyone in the clinical field has been heavily exposed to the eclectic "team" approach to therapy of the child guidance movement, and the somewhat similar eclecticism of the Adolf Meyers - Hopkins school of thought, these eclectic viewpoint have perhaps not been so fruitful in therapy and that little from these sources has been retained in the non-directive approach. It might also have been pointed out that in its basic trend away from guiding and directing the client. the non-directive approach is deeply rooted in practical clinical experience, and is in accord with the experience of most clinical workers, so much so that one of the commonest reactions of experienced therapists is that "You have crystallized and put into words something that I have been groping toward in my own experience for a long time."

Such an analysis, such a tracing or root ideas, needs to be made, but I doubt my own ability to make it. I am also doubtful that anyone who is deeply concerned with a new development knows with any degree of accuracy where his ideas came from.

Consequently I am, in this presentation. Adopting a third pathway. While I shall bring in a brief description of process and procedure. and while I shall acknowledge in a general way our indebtedness to many root sources, and shall recognize the many common elements shared by client-centered therapy and other approaches, I believe it will be to our mutual advantage if I stress primarily those aspects in which nondirective therapy differs most sharply and deeply from other therapeutic procedures. I hope to point out some of the basically significant ways in which the client-centered viewpoint differs from others, not only in its present principles, but in the wider divergencies which are implied by the projection of its central principles.

THE PREDICTABLE PROCESS OF CLIENT-CENTERED THERAPY

The first of the three distinctive elements of client-centered therapy to which I wish to call your attention is the predictability of the therapeutic process in this approach. We find, both clinically and statistically, that a predictable pattern of therapeutic development takes place. The assurance which we feel about this was brought home to me recently when I played a recorded first interview for the graduate students in our practicum immediately after it was recorded, pointing out the characteristic aspects, and agreeing to play later interviews for them to let them see the later phases of the counseling process. The fact that I knew with assurance what the later pattern would be before it had occurred only struck me as I thought about the incident. We have become clinically so accustomed to this predictable quality that we take it for granted. Perhaps a brief summarized description of this therapeutic process will indicate those elements of which we feel sure.

It may be said that we now know how to initiate a complex and predictable chain of events in dealing with the maladjusted individual, a chain of events which is therapeutic, and

41

which operates effectively in problem situations of the most diverse type. This predictable chain of events may come about through the use of language as in counseling, through symbolic language, as in play therapy, through disguised language as in drama or puppet therapy. It is effective in dealing with individual situations, and also in small group situations.

It is possible to state with some exactness the conditions which must be met in order to initiate and carry through this releasing therapeutic experience. Below are listed in brief form the conditions which seem to be necessary, and the therapeutic results which occur.

This experience which releases the growth forces within the individual will come about in most cases if the following elements are present.

1. If the counselor operates on the principle that the individual is basically responsible for himself, and is willing for the individual to keep that responsibility.

2. If the counselor operates on the principle that the client has a strong drive to become mature, socially adjusted. independent, productive, and relies on this force, not on his own powers, for therapeutic change.

3. If the counselor creates a warm and permissive atmosphere in which the individual is free to bring out any attitudes and feelings which he may have, no matter how unconventional, absurd, or contradictory these attitudes may be. The client is as free to withhold expression as he is to give expression to his feelings.

4. If the limits which are set are simple limits set on behavior, and not limits set on attitudes. (This applies mostly to children. The child may not be permitted to break a window or leave the room. but he is free to feel like breaking a window, and the feeling is fully accepted. The adult client may not be permitted more than an hour for an interview, but there is full acceptance of his desire to claim more time.)

5. If the therapist uses only those procedures and techniques in the interview which convey his deep understanding of the emotionalized attitudes expressed and his acceptance of them. This understanding is perhaps best conveyed by a sensitive reflection and clarification of the client's attitudes. The counselor's acceptance involves neither approval nor disapproval.

6. If the counselor refrains from any expression or action which is contrary to the preceding principles. This means reframing from questioning, probing, blame, interpretation, advice, suggestion, persuasion, reassurance

If these conditions are met. then it may be said with assurance that in the great majority of cases the following results will take place.

1. The client will express deep and motivating attitudes.

2. The client will explore his own attitudes and reactions more fully than he has previously done and will come to be aware of aspects of his attitudes which he has previously denied.

3. He will arrive at a clearer conscious realization of his motivating attitudes and will accept himself more completely. This realization and this acceptance will include attitudes previously denied. He may or may not verbalize this clearer conscious understanding of himself and his behavior.

4. In the light of his clearer perception of himself he will choose, on his own initiative and on his own responsibility, new goal which are more satisfying than his maladjusted goals.

5. He will choose to behave in a different fashion in order to reach these goals, and this new behavior will be in the direction of greater psychological growth and maturity. It will also be more spontaneous and less tense, more in harmony with social needs of others, will represent a more realistic and more comfortable adjustment to life. It will be more integrated than his former behavior. It will be a step forward in the life of the individual.

The best scientific description of this process is that supplied by Snyder. Analyzing a number of cases with strictly objective research techniques, Snyder has discovered that the development in these cases is roughly parallel, that the initial phase of catharsis is replaced by a phase in which insight becomes the most significant element, and this in turn by a phase marked by the increase in positive choice and action

Clinically, we know that sometimes this process is relatively shallow, involving primarily a fresh reorientation to an immediate problem, and in other instances so deep as to involve a complete reorientation of personality. It is recognizably the same process whether it involves a girl who is unhappy in a dormitory and is able in three interviews to see something of her childishness and dependence, and to take steps in a mature direction, or whether it involves a young man who is on the edge of a schizophrenic break, and who

44

in thirty interviews works out deep insights in relation to his desire for his father's death, and his possessive and incestuous impulses toward is mother, and who not only takes new steps but rebuilds his whole personality in the process. Whether shallow or deep, it is basically the same.

We are coming to recognize with assurance characteristic aspects of each phase of the process. We know that the catharsis involves a gradual and more complete expression of emotionalized attitudes. We know that characteristically the conversation goes from superficial problems and attitudes to deeper problems and attitudes. We know that this process of exploration gradually unearths relevant attitudes which have been denied to consciousness. We recognize too that the process of achieving insight is likely to involve more adequate facing of reality as it exists within the self, as well as external reality; that it involves the relating of problems to each other, the perception of patterns of behavior; that it involves the acceptance of hitherto denied elements of the self, and a reformulating of the self-concept; and that it involves the making of new plans.

In the final phase we know that the choice of new ways of behaving will be in conformity with the newly organized concept of the self; that first steps in putting these plans into action will be small but symbolic; that the individual will feel only a minimum degree of confidence that he can put his plans into effect, that later steps implement more and more completely the new concept of self, and that this process continues beyond the conclusion of the therapeutic interviews.

If these statements seem to contain too much assurance, to sound "too good to be true," I can only say that for many of them we now have research backing, and that as rapidly as possible we are developing our research to bring all phases of the process under objective scrutiny. Those of us working clinically with client-centered therapy regard this predictability as a settled characteristic, even though we recognize that additional research will be necessary to fill out the picture more completely.

It is the implication of this predictability which is startling. Whenever, in science, a predictable process has been discovered, it has been found possible to use it as a starting point for a whole chain of discoveries. We regard this as not only entirely possible, but inevitable, with regard to this predictable process in therapy. Hence, we regard this orderly and predictable nature of nondirective therapy as one of its most distinctive and significant points of difference from other approaches. Its importance lies not only in the fact that it is a present difference. but in the fact that it points toward a sharply different future, in which scientific exploration of this known chain of events should lead to many new discoveries, developments. and applications.

THE DISCOVERY OF THE CAPACITY OF THE CLIENT

Naturally the question is raised, what is the reason for this predictability in a type of therapeutic procedure in which the therapist serves only a catalytic function? Basically the reason for the predictability of the therapeutic process lies in the discovery - and I use that word intentionally - that within the client reside constructive forces whose strength and uniformity have been either entirely unrecognized or grossly underestimated. It is the clearcut and disciplined reliance by the therapist upon those forces within the client, which seems to account for the orderliness of the therapeutic process, and its consistency from one client to the next.

46

I mentioned that I regarded this as a discovery. I would like to amplify that statement. We have known for centuries that catharsis and emotional release were helpful. Many new methods have been and are being developed to bring about release, but the principle is not new. Likewise, we have known since Freud's time that insight, if it is accepted and assimilated by the client, is therapeutic. The principle is not new. Likewise we have realized that revised action patterns, new ways of behaving, may come about as a result of insight. The principle is not new.

But we have not known or recognized that in most if not all individuals there exist growth forces, tendencies toward self-actualization, which may act as the sole motivation for therapy. We have not realized that under suitable psychological conditions these forces bring about emotional release in those areas and at those rates which are most beneficial to the individual. These forces drive the individual to explore his own attitudes and his relationship to reality. and to explore these areas effectively. We have not realized that the individual is capable of exploring his attitudes and feelings, including those which have been denied to consciousness, at a rate which does not cause panic, and to the depth required for comfortable adjustment. The individual is capable of discovering and perceiving, truly and spontaneously, the interrelationships between his own attitudes, and the relationship of himself to reality. The individual has the capacity and the strength to devise, quite unguided, the steps which will lead him to a more mature and more comfortable relationship to his reality. It is the gradual and increasing recognition of these capacities within the individual by the client-centered therapist that rates, I believe, the term discovery. All of these capacities I have described are released in the individual if a suitable psychological atmosphere is provided.

47

There has, of course, been lip service paid to the strength of the client, and the need of utilizing the urge toward independence which exists in the client. Psychiatrists, analysts, and especially social case workers have stressed this point. Yet it is clear from what is said, and even more clear from the case material cited. that this confidence is a very limited confidence. It is a confidence that the client can take over, if guided by the expert, a confidence that the client can assimilate insight if it is first, given to him by the expert, can make choices providing guidance is given at crucial points. It is, in short, the same sort of attitude which the mother has toward the adolescent. that she believes in his capacity to make his own decisions and guide his own life, providing he takes the directions of which she approves.

This is very evident in the latest book on psychoanalysis by Alexander and French. Although many of the former views and practices of psychoanalysis are discarded, and the procedures are far more nearly in line with those of nondirective therapy, it is still the therapist who is definitely in control. He gives the insights. he is ready to guide at crucial points. Thus while the authors state that the aim of the therapist is to free the patient to develop his capacities, and to increase his ability to satisfy his needs in ways acceptable to himself and society; and while they speak of the basic conflict between competition and cooperation as one which the individual must settle for himself; and speak of the integration of new insight as a normal function of the ego, it is clear when they speak of procedures that they have no confidence that the client has the capacity to do any of these things. For in practice, "As soon as the therapist takes the more active role we advocate, systematic planning becomes imperative. In addition to the original decision as to the particular sort of strategy to be employed in the treatment of any case, we recommend the conscious use of various tech-

48

niques in a flexible manner, shifting tactics to fit the particular needs of the moment. Among these modifications of the standard technique are; using not only the method of free association but interviews of a more direct character, manipulating the frequency of the interviews, giving directives to the patient concerning his daily life, employing interruptions of long or short duration in preparation for ending the treatment, regulating the transference relation-hip to meet the specific needs of the case, and making use of real-life experiences as an integral part of therapy". At least this leaves no doubt as to whether it is the client's or the therapist's hour; it is clearly the latter. The capacities which the client is to develop are clearly not to be developed in the therapeutic sessions.

The client-centered therapist stands at an opposite pole, both theoretically and practically. He has learned that the constructive forces in the individual can be trusted. and that the more deeply they are relied upon, the more deeply they are released. He has come to build his procedures upon these hypotheses, which are rapidly becoming established as facts; that the client knows the areas of concern which he is ready to explore; that the client is the best judge as to the most desirable frequency of interviews; that the client can lead the way more efficiently than the therapist into deeper concerns; that the client will protect himself from panic by ceasing to explore an area which is becoming too painful; that the client can and will uncover all the repressed elements which it is necessary to uncover in order to build a comfortable adjustment; that the client can achieve for himself far truer and more sensitive and accurate insights than can possibly be given to him; that the client is capable of translating these insights into constructive behavior which weigh his own needs and desires realistically against the demands of society; that the client knows when therapy is completed and he is ready to cope with life independently. Only one condition is necessary for all these forces to be released, and that is the proper psychological atmosphere between client and therapist.

Our case records and increasingly our research bear out these statements. One might suppose that there would be a generally favorable reaction to this discovery, since it amounts in effect to tapping great reservoirs of hitherto little-used energy. Quite the contrary is true, however, in professional groups. There is no other aspect of client-centered therapy which comes under such vigorous attack. It seems to be genuinely disturbing to many professional people to entertain the thought that this client upon whom they have been exercising their professional skill actually knows more about his inner psychological self than they can possibly know, and that he possesses constructive strengths which make the constructive push by the therapist seem puny indeed by comparison. The willingness fully to accept this strength of the client, with all the re-orientation of therapeutic procedure which it implies, is one of the ways in which client-centered therapy differs most sharply from other therapeutic approaches.

THE CLIENT-CENTERED NATURE OF THE THERAPEUTIC RELATIONSHIP

The third distinctive feature of this type of therapy is the character of the relationship between therapist and client. Unlike other therapies in which the skills of the therapist are to be exercised upon the client. in this approach the skills of the therapist are focused upon creating a psychological atmosphere in which the client can work. If the counselor can create a relationship permeated by warmth, understanding, safety from any type of attack, no matter how trivial, and basic acceptance of the person as he is, then the client will drop his natural defensiveness and use the situation. As we have puzzled over the characteristics of a successful therapeutic relationship, we have come to feel that the sense of communication is very important. If the client feels that he is actually communicating his present attitudes, superficial, confused, or conflicted as they may be, and that his communication is understood rather than evaluated in any way, then he is freed to communicate more deeply. A relationship in which the client thus feels that he is communicating is almost certain to be fruitful.

All of this means a drastic reorganization in the counselor's thinking, particularly if he has previously utilized other approaches. He gradually learns that the statement that the time is to be "the client's hour" means just that, and that his biggest task is to make it more and more deeply true.

Perhaps something of the characteristics of the relationship may be suggested by excerpts from a paper written by a young minister who has spent several months learning client-centered counseling procedures.

"Because the client-centered, nondirective counseling approach has been rather carefully defined and clearly illustrated, it gives the "Illusion of Simplicity." The technique seems deceptively easy to master. Then you begin to practice. A word is wrong here and there. You don't quite reflect feeling, but reflect content instead. It is difficult to handle questions; you are tempted to interpret. Nothing seems so serious that further practice won't correct it. Perhaps you are having trouble playing two roles - that of minister and that of counselor. Bring up the question in class and the matter is solved again with a deceptive ease.

But these apparently minor errors and a certain woodenness of response seem exceedingly persistent.

"Only gradually does it dawn that if the technique is true it demands a feeling of warmth. You begin to feel that the attitude is the thing. Every little word is not so important if you have the correct accepting and permissive attitude toward the client. So you bear down on the permissiveness and acceptance. You will permiss and accept and reflect the client, if it kills you!

But you still have those troublesome questions from the client. He simply doesn't know the next step. He asks you to give him a hint, some possibilities, after all you are expected to know something, else why is he here! As a minister, you ought to have some convictions about what people should believe, how they should act. As a counselor, you should know something about removing this obstacle - you ought to have the equivalent of the surgeon's knife and use it. Then you begin to wonder. The technique is good, but...does it go far enough! does it really work on clients? is it right to leave a person helpless, when you might show him the way out?

Here it seems to me is the crucial point. "Narrow is the gate" and hard the path from here on. So one else can give satisfying answers and even the instructors seem frustrating because they appear not to be helpful in your specific case. For here is demanded of you what no other person can do or point out - and that is to rigorously scrutinize yourself and your attitudes towards others. Do you believe that all people truly have a creative potential in them? That each person is a unique individual and that he alone can work out his own individuality? Or do you really believe that some persons are of "negative value" and others are weak and must be led and taught by "wiser," "stronger" people.

"You begin to see that there is nothing compartmentalized about this method of counseling. It is not just counseling, because it demands the most exhaustive, penetrating, and comprehensive consistency. In other methods you can shape tools, pick them up for use when you will. But when genuine acceptance and permissiveness are your tools it requires nothing less than the whole complete personality. And to grow oneself is the most demanding of all."

He goes on to discuss the notion that the counselor must be restrained and "self-denying." He concludes that this is a mistaken notion.

"Instead of demanding less of the counselor's personality in the situation, client-centered counseling in some ways demands more. It demands discipline, not restraint. It calls for the utmost in sensitivity, appreciative awareness. channeled and disciplined. It demands that the counselor put all he has of these precious qualities into the situation, but in a disciplined, refined manner. It is restraint only in the sense that the counselor does not express himself in certain areas that he may use himself in others.

"Even this is deceptive, however. It is not so much restraint in any area as it is a focusing, sensitizing one's energies and personality in the direction of an appreciative and understanding attitude."

As time has gone by we have come to put increasing stress upon the "client-centeredness" of the relationship, because it is more effective the more completely the counselor concentrates upon trying to understand the client as the client seems to himself. As I look back upon some of our earlier published cases - the case of Herbert Bryan in my book, or Snyder's case of Mr. M. - I realize that we have gradually dropped the vestiges of subtle directiveness which are all too evident in those cases. We have come to recognize that if we can provide understanding of the way the client seems to himself at this moment, he can do the rest. The therapist must lay aside his preoccupation with diagnosis and his diagnostic shrewdness, must discard his tendency to make professional evaluations, must cease his endeavors to formulate an accurate prognosis, must give up the temptation subtly to guide the individual, and must concentrate on one purpose only; that of providing deep understanding and acceptance of the attitudes consciously held at this moment by the client as he explores step by step into the dangerous areas which he has been denying to consciousness.

I trust it is evident from this description that this type of relationship can exist only if the counselor is deeply and genuinely able to adopt these attitudes. Client-centered counseling, if it is to be effective, cannot be a trick or a tool. It is not a subtle way of guiding the client while pretending to let him guide himself. To be effective, it must be genuine. It is this sensitive and sincere "client-centeredness" in the therapeutic relationship that I regard as the third characteristic of nondirective therapy which sets it distinctively apart from other approaches.

SOME IMPLICATIONS

Although the client-centered approach had its origin purely within the limits of the psychological clinic, it is proving to have implications, often of a startling nature, for very diverse fields of effort. I should like to suggest a few of these present and potential implications.

In the field of psychotherapy itself, it leads to conclusions that seem distinctly heretical. It appears evident that training and practice in therapy should probably precede training in the field of diagnosis. Diagnostic knowledge and skill is not necessary for good therapy, a statement which sounds like blasphemy to many, and if the professional worker, whether psychiatrist, psychologist or caseworker, received training in therapy first he would learn psychological dynamics in a truly dynamic fashion, and would acquire a professional humility and willingness to learn from his client which is today all too rare.

The viewpoint appears to have implications for medicine. It has fascinated me to observe that when a prominent allergist began to use client-centered therapy for the treatment of non-specific allergies, he found not only very good therapeutic results, but the experience began to affect his whole medical practice. It has gradually meant the reorganization of his office procedure. He has given his nurses a new type of training in understanding the patient. He has decided to have all medical histories taken by a nonmedical person trained in nondirective techniques, in order to get a true picture of the client's feelings and attitudes toward himself and his health, uncluttered by the bias and diagnostic evaluation which is almost inevitable when a medical person takes the history and unintentionally distorts the material by his premature judgments. He has found these histories much more helpful to the physicians than those taken by physicians.

The client-centered viewpoint has already been shown to have significant implications for the field of survey interviewing and public opinion study. Use of such techniques by Likert, Lazarsfeld, and others has meant the elimination of much of the factor of bias in such studies.

This approach has also, we believe, deep implications for the handling of social and group conflicts, as I have pointed out in another paper. Our work in applying a client-centered viewpoint to group therapy situations, while still in its early stages, leads us to feel that a significant clue to the constructive solution of interpersonal and intercultural frictions in the group may be in our hands. Application of these procedures to staff groups, to inter-racial groups, to groups with personal problems and tensions, is under way.

In the field of education, too, the client-centered approach is finding significant application. The work of Cantor, a description of which will soon be published, is outstanding in this connection, but a number of teachers are finding that these methods, designed for therapy, produce a new type of educational process, an independent learning which is highly desirable, and even a reorientation of individual direction which is very similar to the results of individual or group therapy.

Even in the realm of our philosophical orientation, the client-centered approach has its deep implications. I should like to indicate this by quoting briefly from a previous paper.

As we examine and try to evaluate our clinical experience with client-centered therapy, the phenomenon of the reorganization of attitudes and the redirection of behavior by the individual assumes greater and greater importance. This phenomenon seems to find inadequate explanation in terms of the determinism which is the predominant philosophical background of most psychological work. The capacity of the individual to reorganize his attitudes and behavior in ways not determined by external factors nor by previous elements in his own experience, but determined by his own insight into those factors, is an impressive capacity. It involves a basic spontaneity which we have been loathe to admit into our scientific thinking.

The clinical experience could be summarized by saying that the behavior of the human organism may be determined by the influences to which it has been exposed, but it may also be determined by the creative and integrative insight of the organism itself. This ability of the person to discover new meaning in the forces which impinge upon him and in the past experiences which have been controlling him, and the ability to alter consciously his behavior in the light of this new meaning, has a profound significance for our thinking which has not been fully realized. We need to revise the philosophical basis of our work to a point where it can admit that forces exist within the individual which can exercise a spontaneous and significant influence upon behavior which is not predictable through knowledge of prior influences and conditionings. The forces released through a catalytic process of therapy are not adequately accounted for by a knowledge of the individual's previous conditionings, but only if we grant the presence of a spontaneous force within the organism which has the capacity of integration and redirection. This capacity for volitional control is a force which we must take into account in any psychological equation.

So we find an approach which began merely as a way of dealing with problems of human maladjustment forcing us into a revaluation of our basic philosophical concepts.

SUMMARY

I hope that throughout this paper I have managed to convey what is my own conviction, that what we now know or think we know about a client-centered approach is only a

57

beginning, only the opening of a door beyond which we are beginning to see some very challenging roads, some fields rich with opportunity. It is the facts of our clinical and research experience which keep pointing forward into new and exciting possibilities. Yet whatever the future may hold, it appears already clear that we are dealing with materials of a new and significant nature, which demand the most openminded and thorough exploration. If our present formulations of those facts are correct, then we would say that some important elements already stand out; that certain basic attitudes and skills can create a psychological atmosphere which releases, frees, and utilizes deep strengths in the client; that these strengths and capacities are more sensitive and more rugged than hitherto supposed; and that they are released in an orderly and predictable process which may prove as significant a basic fact in social science as some of the laws and predictable processes in the physical sciences.

SELECTED REFERENCES

1. ALEXANDER, F. AND FRENCH, T. Psychoanalytic Therapy. New York: Ronald Press, 1946.

2. ALLEN, F. Psychotherapy with Children. New York: Norton, 1942.

3. CANTOR, N. Employee Counseling. New York: McGraw-Hill Book Company.

4. CANTOR, N. The Dynamics of Learning. (unpublished mss.) University of Buffalo, 1943.

5. CURRAN, C. A. Personality Factors in Counseling. New York: Grune and Stratton, 1945.

6. RANK, O. Will Therapy. New York: Alfred A. Knopf 1936.

7. ROGERS, C. R. "Counseling", Review of Educational Research. April 1945 (Vol. 15), pp. 135-163.

8. ROGERS, C. R. Counseling and Psychotherapy. New York: Houghton Mifflin Co., 1942.

9. ROGERS, C`. R. The implications of nondirective therapy for the handling of social conflicts. Paper given to a seminar of the Bureau of Intercultural Education, New York City, Feb. 18, 1946.

10. ROGERS. C. R. AND WALLEN, J. L. Counseling with Returned Servicemen. New York: McGraw-Hill, 1946.

11. SNYDER, W. U. "An Investigation of the Nature of Non-Directive Psychotherapy." Journal of General Psychology. Vol. 33, 1945. pp.193-223.

12. TAFT, J. The Dynamics of Therapy in a Controlled Relationship. New York: Macmillan, 1933.

The Psychology on Kindle Collection

The psychology on kindle collection forms part of an initiative to make important, insightful and engaging psychology publications widely available. The collection includes articles written by the most eminent and influential psychologists of the 20th century (Freud, Bandura, Jung, Maslow, Vygotsky, Skinner, Rogers etc.) See following link for full details.

www.all-about-psychology.com/psychology-on-kindle.html

Psychology Student Guide

Drawing on my experience as both a student and also a University lecturer in Psychology, the Psychology Student Guide is designed for people who want to learn more about what psychology actually is, people who are thinking of studying psychology and people who are currently undergraduate psychology students. See following link for full details.

http://bit.ly/PsychStudentGuide

Wishing you all the very best

David Webb BSc (hons), MSc

Made in United States
Troutdale, OR
01/03/2024

16677199R00035